THE SPIRIT OF

NORFOLK

TERENCE J BURCHELL

HALSGROVE

First published in Great Britain in 2007

British Library Cataloguing-in-Publication Data
A CIP record for this title is available from the British Library

ISBN 978 1 84114 655 3

HALSGROVE
Halsgrove House
Ryelands Farm Industrial Estate
Bagley Green, Wellington
Somerset TA21 9PZ
Tel: 01823 653777
Fax: 01823 216796
email: sales@halsgrove.com
website: www.halsgrove.com

Printed and bound by D'Auria Industrie Grafiche Spa, Italy

Introduction

If you live in Norfolk I hope this book will evoke happy memories of this most beautiful county. Norfolk is so diverse in its character. Its sweeping coastline, the unique landscapes of the Broads, the individuality of its villages and towns, each add to the charm of why, those who reside here, hold it so dear.

If you are a visitor, or perhaps may never have been to Norfolk, I hope this book will whet your appetite to explore further, not just the attractive holiday seaside resorts, but the pretty villages and quiet country lanes. These photographs reflect the county I have come to know and love over forty years, and where I know you will also find a warm welcome.

Terence J. Burchell

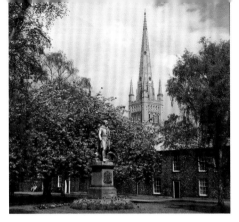

The City of Norwich is not missed by the touch of Spring. The Cathedral
and the surrounding Close are tinged with colour, with the statue
of Wellington rising proudly above the beds of flowers.

Opposite page:
This scene is taken from Acle Bridge looking into the rising sun
which casts a romantic glow over the moored pleasure boats
alongside the banks of the River Bure.

The *Albion* passes by a young angler sitting on the bank of the Yare.

Opposite page:
Ashwellthorpe, a village close to Wymondham, contains some pretty cottages.

The *Olive* and *Norada* are seen here passing each other on
the River Yare at Whittlingham, just outside Norwich.

Opposite page:
Almost in the centre of Norwich the River Wensum passes modern developments, but
the scene is still attractive with an old day launch having just passed under Fye Bridge.

Swan, geese and pleasure craft stand side by side at Salhouse Broad.

Opposite page:
Pull's Ferry, named after one
of the ferrymen who once
took people across the river here.

This Broad at Filby attracts all the usual water activities, but rarely gets crowded.

Opposite page:
What waterfalls there are in the county are not spectacular. Although this one is certainly small it is set under trees on the River Wensum near Swanton Morley and makes for a pretty picture.

Blickling Hall has a most attractive lake in the grounds on the edge of Blickling Park.

Opposite page:
Lyndford Hall is found between Thetford and Swaffham.

A horse calmly contemplates the scene, while ducks enjoy the Glaven as it gently flows towards Cley-next-the-Sea.

Opposite page:
This horse and rider create a splash in the still waters of the ford at Glandford on the River Glaven.

Here, at Thorpe, near Norwich, swans eagerly await food while the pleasure Wherries, *Olive* and *Norada*, their white sails echoing the swans' plumage, sail by.

From the top of St Helen's Church in the village of Ranworth you can get views of the Broads –
if you can climb the 89 steps, two ladders and a trapdoor that lead to the viewing platform.
It is certainly worth the effort for this view of Ranworth Broad and beyond.

St Benet's Abbey stands on the banks of the
River Bure between Horning and Thurne.

Opposite page:
On the River Wissey at Whittington canal boats, now used as houseboats, are
moored against the bank where the weeping willows bend down towards the water.

Catching crabs from the waters of the harbour is a popular and pleasurable pastime for children and adults alike!

Opposite page:
At Brancaster Staithe you can find fishing boats and private sailing yachts settling into the mud where the tide has receded, leaving just a trickle of water running away along winding channels.

23

Blakeney, another very popular Summer destination for those who prefer rather quieter holidays. Here sailing, painting or just walking and enjoying the views is the order of the day.

It is from Blakeney or nearby Moreston Quay that you can take one of several boats that chug their way out to Blakeney Point to give visitors the chance to watch the Grey Seals as they either laze on the sand or swim around watching the passing boats.

This hill is known as the Beeston 'Bump', lying at Beeston Regis.

Opposite page:
Sheringham is a larger town. The area is well known for its crabs and other shellfish and these can be bought freshly caught from the North Sea. Here, two local fisherman discuss their catch.

From the top of the 'Bump' can be clearly seen, in one direction Sheringham…

...and, in the other direction, West Runton with its 'town' of caravans. Beyond in the far distance is Cromer.

The Lighthouse at Happisburgh, with St Mary's Church
echoing its shape pointing to the sky, is some
distance inland from the crumbling cliffs.

Opposite page:
The front at Cromer boasts a handsome pier with, at its far end,
a theatre which hosts many shows throughout the year.

Great Yarmouth, the largest of the Norfolk coastal resorts, has many and varied attractions, from its piers to the Pleasure Beach of noisy, colourful rides and sideshows. Even here, however,some people can find a peaceful place to sit.

Cley's eighteenth-century windmill stands next to the Glaven. It may be recognised by many as one of the scenes from television with the balloon floating across the marshland.

A delightful scene of anglers in front of a white-painted windpump standing out against the brilliant blue sky.

Opposite page:
Norfolk has a great number of wind-powered machines situated in a variety of buildings, many mistaken for windmills, when they could well be windpumps. On the River Thurne at Thurne Dyke stands one of the most attractive wind drainage pumps.

Close now to the border with Suffolk, and just a
short distance from Scole and Diss, is Billingford Windmill,
here standing with its face to the sun.

Opposite page:
Clouds gather over Horsey Mill, which
stands not far from Winterton-on-Sea.

Not all mills relied on
the wind for operation.
At Little Cressingham,
near to Swaffham,
this mill has been operated
by either wind, water or
oil in its lifetime.

Opposite page:
Every year throughout the
area demonstrations take
place of old machinery that
once was a common sight
on our farms. Here at
Banham a crowd gathers to
watch corn being threshed
in the old fashioned way.

Union Farm run by the Norfolk Rural Life Museum at Gressenhall where the
animals and implements of the 1920s can be seen still working.
Opposite page:
Standing patiently, this heavy horse, once a regular sight in the fields,
again becomes part of a farming scene rarely observed today.

Sugar beet is one of the most important crops in Norfolk. There are a number of sugar beet factories in the area, the largest being situated at Whissington producing many tons of sugar.

Opposite page:
In high Summer this cottage looks out across the Common with its masses of wild flowers and tall grasses.

Cottage gardens can still be found that reminds one of scenes that might only be found in paintings. This garden at Intwood is certainly one.

Opposite page:
Colour is everywhere.
Rape gives a carpet of yellow beneath a Norfolk sky at Hethel.

Not far up the coast, taken
from a high point, this time
at Salthouse Heath, is this
view of Salthouse and
the church of St Nicholas.

Opposite page:
The Poppy is one of the
most popular of flowers,
whether in small bunches or,
as here, in a great swathe
in a field at East Carleton.

This hill at Quidenham was believed to be the resting place of Queen Boadicea (or Boudicca).

Opposite page:
Local Museum, Dereham.

49

The Priory at Castle Acre was founded by William de Warrene.
Standing in approximately 36 acres it is kept in remarkably good condition.

Throughout the county ruins of ancient fortified houses and castles can be seen. Great Yarmouth has traces of eleven towers that were part of its walled defence. The north-west tower stands alone beside the river Bure.

Churches, it seems, can sometimes come along in twos! Here are two in the same churchyard. They are St Mary's of Reepham and St Michael and All Angels of Whitwell, although only one is now used for services.

Opposite page:
Caister Castle, inland from Caister-on-Sea, built by
Sir John Fastolfe who led the English archers at Agincourt.

Heydon Hall situated in a lovely parkland estate.

Opposite page:
Here, at Burnham Overy, are some fine examples of the cobbled houses
found in the county, especially along the North Norfolk coast.

This excellent example of a market cross stands in the centre of New Buckenham on the B1113. One of the wooden posts still retains the irons used to hold ne'erdowells during their time of penitence.

Opposite page:
Anna Sewell, authoress of Black Beauty, was born at Great Yarmouth into a Quaker family. Anna's birthplace is now a small restaurant.

In Thetford Forest the golden leaves still on the trees are contrasted against the evergreen pines that make up the main part of the forest.

Opposite page:
East Carleton. Winter's grip has fallen on the trees and the surrounding countryside. Although the lake has not quite frozen it seems that it will not be long before the ducks are walking on the ice that will cover the water.

In the fields and lanes surrounding Mulbarton village hoar frost etches the trees against a cold and clear blue sky.

Opposite page:
As the winter sun dips towards the horizon it suddenly bursts through the clouds, silhouetting a derelict windpump that stands forlornly in the middle of marshland near Hickling.

The City of Norwich glows in the light from the setting sun.

Opposite page:
Now the sun struggles to pierce through the mist that covers Mulbarton Common.

Sunset, finally, at Heacham. It is at Heacham that John Rolfe married
his bride Pocahontas in 1614. I wonder, did they stand looking
out at such a magnificent end to a beautiful day?